52-Week Devotional Journal for Grief

52-WEEK DEVOTIONAL
JOURNAL
FOR
GRIEF

Prompts and Prayers for
Navigating Loss

DEBBRA SELL BRONSTAD, LMFT

**ROCKRIDGE
PRESS**

Interior and Cover Designer: Sean Doyle/Chiaka John
Art Producer: Melissa Malinowsky
Editor: Mo Mozuch
Production Editor: Jael Fogle
Production Manager: Holly Haydash

All illustrations used under license from iStock

Paperback ISBN: 978-1-63807-654-4
R0

To Mom, Hazel, Grandma, and Darelyn: I didn't have a clue about how to do grief when you went to heaven. I miss you.

To Chris: Thank you for believing in the vision and for providing the best writer support ever!

To Gay: Thank you for patiently listening to my ups and downs for 30 years.

To Matthew, Kaylin, Jacob, Nolan, and Cole: You light up my life and make me smile. Thanks for bringing me home.

I thank God for the gifts you are to me. I love you all.

CONTENTS

INTRODUCTION

Halfway through my graduate program in clinical psychology, a dear friend and mentor passed away. A year later, her husband died just before Thanksgiving and final exams. I tried to stay busy enough to outpace the pain of losing people who were like parents to me. In my training to counsel others, I realized I had seen only one paragraph in a textbook about dealing with grief.

My background is in church ministry. I spent years helping people find peace and calm through encounters with Jesus during inner healing prayer ministry. Almost everyone I ministered to shared grief of some sort, even if it wasn't due to a death. According to the Grief Recovery Institute, grief is the normal and natural human reaction to loss or change. We experience grief as the conflicting feelings caused by the end of or change in a familiar pattern of behavior. I wondered if I was *doing* grief right. I was working, going to school full-time, and doing homework in the remaining hours. When I tried to get quiet with the Lord, I was overwhelmed with pain, so I avoided that. The stress increased, and I began experiencing insomnia, mood swings, weight gain, and fatigue.

In a used bookstore one day, a little book jumped off the shelf. The title told me there was hope for recovery. I attended a training to help others deal with grief. Unexpectedly, the first half of the training took me through exercises to work through my own pain. Afterward, I was grateful to share with the group about losing my mom through divorce, the death of my stepmom who raised me, and other losses. I realized how many losses I had been holding on to since childhood. Over that weekend, I relinquished burdens about many things I couldn't change. Since 2010, as a marriage and family therapist, I have been helping individuals, groups, and families make peace with their grief, adjusting their lives to the new normal.

In this devotional journal I share many of the lessons I learned in my own grief journey, as well as from counseling others toward healing. This book is for anyone who is looking for scripture-based guidance for reflecting on and managing their grief. It is also a tool to help you spend time with God and to strengthen your faith as you walk through one of life's most difficult experiences. Grief involves meditating on the quality of your relationship with the person who died. I invite you to consider those memories in the presence of the Lord.

HOW TO USE
THIS BOOK

This book is designed for you to read, pray, and journal every week for a year. Work through the readings and questions once a week or reflect on them a little bit each day. Feel free to start with the topics that catch your attention first. There is no need to go in order. Whatever helps you spend time with God will be the best way for you.

Since grief is unpredictable and unique, it can be helpful to note your experience over time. Roughly every 10 or 11 weeks, you will reflect on your journey in the *Observing Grief* sections, which will also help you look forward to what's ahead. The *Observing Grief* sections include activities for quieting yourself, so you can better listen for God's response as you share your pain with Him. Some activities include visualization exercises, because pictures are a language of the heart and can help you acknowledge and process your feelings. Other mindfulness practices can help you identify and release emotions. A comfortable seat in a chair or on the floor in a place with few distractions will help. You can focus on breathing in a steady rhythmic pattern (it is okay if you lose focus) and release mental distractions by verbally letting them go or writing them down. The goal of quieting yourself is to focus on what is happening in your heart and spirit. My prayer is that you will connect with the Lord in a fruitful and intimate way.

Please also note that while this book should not be used as a replacement for professional therapy, it can be used to support your therapy work.

OPENING PRAYER

Lord, thank You that You know my pain. Thank You for Your promise to never leave me. Please help me know more of Your love for me. I bring my broken heart to You. Help me grow and heal in this season, in Jesus's name. Amen.

Are There Really Stages of Grief?

Blessed are those who mourn,
for they will be comforted.

MATTHEW 5:4

The phrase *stages of grief*, coined by Elisabeth Kübler-Ross, has permeated our culture, solidifying the belief that grief progresses through a predictable five-point sequence: denial, anger, bargaining, depression, and acceptance. However, the reality is that grief is much more complex. David Kessler, who co-authored *On Grief and Grieving* with Kübler-Ross, writes about the stages: "They were never meant to help tuck messy emotions into neat packages. They are responses to loss that many people have, but there is not a typical response to loss as there is no typical loss. Our grief is as individual as our lives."

Though grief does not have a timetable, it does have a process, one that can lead to healing. It is healthy and important to understand and nurture that process, which will be unique to your loss. Over time, we reflect on our relationship with our loved one. We remember the positives and the negatives of our experiences together. Because death provokes intense feelings, as our attachment bonds are broken, the experience of grief can affect us physically, emotionally, cognitively, socially, and spiritually. We will explore these symptoms in more depth over the next few weeks.

What does grief feel like to you? How do you experience it?

What questions do you have about the process of grief? What
steps will you take to find answers? How do you hope this journal will help you?

Every Grief Is Different

He heals the brokenhearted and
binds up their wounds.

PSALM 147:3

Nothing rocks our emotional world like grief does. When my
57-year-old stepmom passed away unexpectedly two months
after a cancer diagnosis, I remember feeling deflated. My drive
and motivation disappeared. I told myself for years that my
parents were young and that I had plenty of time to spend with
them in the future. I suddenly regretted missing so many family
gatherings while I lived across the country. As many grieving
people do, I realized nothing would ever be the same.

Others describe grief as feeling like fear and anxiety, loneliness, anger, and/or irritability. Sometimes people feel numb
or empty, or they have a sense of observing themselves, or life,
without participating in it. These, and many other ways grief
may manifest, are normal responses to loss. There are no set
stages or prescribed feelings that always accompany grief,
which is as unique as the people and relationships involved.
People may try to be sympathetic and say "I know how you feel,"
but the reality is they really don't know. They may remember
what they felt like when they were grieving a loss, but that may
or may not be your experience. Every grief is different.

What does grief feel like for you? In what ways is your grief different than you expected or from others' grief you have observed?

....

....

....

....

....

....

....

When you consider God's promise in Psalm 147:3 to heal the bro-kenhearted, what do you believe that could look like for you? Write down your prayer for God's healing work in your heart.

....

....

....

....

....

Physical Symptoms

My flesh and my heart may fail,
but God is the strength of my
heart and my portion forever.
PSALM 73:26

Grief affects the body in countless ways. Examples of physical symptoms of grief include crying, increased or decreased appetite, body aches, fatigue, chest tightness or pain, difficulty breathing, increased inflammation, increased susceptibility to disease due to lowered immunity, feelings of emptiness, insomnia, or anxiety. The stress of grieving can create physical problems that may need medical attention.

It is important to acknowledge your body's relationship to grief, as well as the ways grief can manifest physically; in doing so, you can empower yourself toward one facet of healing. Exercise is a way to relieve stress and anxiety associated with grief. Walking outdoors, swimming, riding a bike, or gentle stretching can all be ways to release the stress in your body. Deep breathing can also help. There are apps available for your smartphone to encourage relaxation through guided meditations and breathing exercises. Be sure to consult your doctor about any new exercise regime or about concerning physical symptoms. Other physical symptoms may simply require that we acknowledge and validate our emotions, so they don't have to express themselves as strongly through our bodies.

What physical symptoms have you noticed since you have been grieving? What types of activities or exercises might alleviate those symptoms?

What strategies could you use to express your feelings more intentionally (e.g., talking to a friend, exercising, journaling, etc.)? Create a plan to acknowledge your feelings this week. Decide on your first steps and write them down.

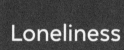

Loneliness

*The Lord bless you and keep you; the
Lord make his face shine on you and
be gracious to you; the Lord turn his
face toward you and give you peace.*

NUMBERS 6:24-26

Loneliness is a unique state of mind in which to develop faith.
It is the desire for someone to turn toward us, to let us know
our existence matters. Now that someone who regularly turned
toward you is gone, the pain and emptiness can be indescrib-
able. There will be times when we feel connected to others who
care, but loneliness isn't always about being alone. We can feel
lonely, even in a crowd, when we don't feel seen or valued. We
can also be alone without feeling lonely.

In times of loneliness, we need faith in God and His Word to
tell us we won't always feel this way. In heaven, we will not be
lonely. When you feel that need to be seen, you can make the
above psalm your prayer. Call on God to ask Him to turn to you
and be gracious to you. He desires to turn toward you.

What are some positive ways that your loved one turned toward you that you miss?

Take a moment to turn toward the lonely part of yourself. Write a note to that part expressing that "you matter." It might start something like this: "It makes sense to me that you feel lonely because..."

The Lord Is My Shepherd

Even though I walk through the
darkest valley, I will fear no evil,
for you are with me; your rod and
your staff, they comfort me.

PSALM 23:4

When we are vulnerable during grief, we need protection and guidance. Our Good Shepherd leads us through life, through the good times and the bad. What would it be like to walk through the valley of the shadow of death and actually fear no evil simply because of the presence of the Lord? The Lord desires to comfort us. He has a special place in His heart for those who acknowledge their needs. Grief has a way of undermining our sense of independence, as well as our belief that we have control over what happens in our lives. In a moment, things that we trusted in and believed to be secure can vanish. The wisest man who ever lived wrote, "It is better to go to a house of mourning than to go to a house of feasting, for death is the destiny of everyone; the living should take this to heart" (Ecclesiastes 7:2). Death refreshes our perspective on life. We realize how vulnerable we are and how fragile life is, but we are also reminded of our capacity to live and love. It helps us not take people and experiences for granted.

In what ways have you noticed God's presence in your life, especially in this season?

_____

_____

_____

_____

_____

_____

How has experiencing the death of your loved one affected your perspective on life? Has anything changed in how you view your relationships? Write your reflections.

_____

_____

_____

_____

_____

_____

_____

_____

Anxiety

Cast all your anxiety on him
because he cares for you.

1 PETER 5:7

Worry can create the illusion that we are working on a problem when, in reality, it is simply a feedback loop, a source of stress that changes nothing. Anxiety is often a cap covering other more vulnerable emotions. It is letting us know that something deeper in the heart needs attention. Anxiety may simply be protecting us from the pain of grief. Or we may not know what it is defending. A path to discovery can be to sit quietly with the discomfort and gently ask the anxiety in our soul questions like, "What are you protecting?" or "What do you need to feel calmer?"

Pat, a client of mine, had a hard time sleeping after his son died in a college hazing incident. As bedtime approached, Pat became anxious and felt his shoulders tense. Work and family responsibilities, and even distractions such as internet surfing, binge-watching TV shows, or playing online games, kept his emotions from surfacing. For many people, bedtime is the first time they get quiet after the busyness of the day. Pat and I discussed some ways to attend to his anxiety and grief intentionally. He began journaling 15 minutes a day about his feelings, acknowledging them and giving them to the Lord in prayer. Eventually, he noticed he was less anxious at bedtime and found it easier to fall asleep.

Make a list of your anxieties. In your imagination, see yourself offering each one to Jesus. Maybe they look like bricks or shopping bags. The point is to put the scene in your mind where He is carrying these burdens and you are not.

Make a note of the times of the day or experiences that you have that tend to lead to anxiety. If you have a conversation with your anxiety, how does it respond?

Exhaustion

He gives strength to the weary and increases the power of the weak. Even youths grow tired and weary, and young men stumble and fall; but those who hope in the Lord will renew their strength. They will soar on wings like eagles; they will run and not grow weary, they will walk and not be faint.

ISAIAH 40:29–31

Do you feel weary sometimes? Grief is exhausting. It robs our vitality for life. Our motivation wanes for doing things we've always done and enjoyed. When we miss someone we love, it can feel like a part of us died with them. We miss who we were when they were around. Life may not interest us as much as it used to. We can feel the fatigue physically, mentally, and in other ways. God promises that when we are weak, He is strong. As we hope in Him, our strength is renewed. Sometimes all we can do is do the next thing, asking for God's strength and guidance.

What are some of the "next things" you need to accomplish? In what ways do you need your strength renewed? How do you express your "hope in the Lord"?

_____

_____

_____

_____

_____

If you could soar through your grief experience, what would you make easier? What would be different than what you are experiencing right now?

_____

_____

_____

_____

_____

_____

_____

Why Can't I Think Straight?

We are hard pressed on every side, but not crushed; perplexed, but not in despair . . .

2 CORINTHIANS 4:8

Grief requires a lot of mental energy. Coming to terms with the fact that someone who has been there for you is no longer there can be distracting. Grievers are often forgetful, unable to remember where they put items, like their keys or their debit card, or where they parked the car. Simple tasks can become confusing and frustrating. Some people, when grieving, catch themselves paused by a memory in the middle of a task, like a potent daydream. In social situations, you might feel like your mind is somewhere else. Decisions can be difficult because the options demand too much energy to consider. When others ask you a question, you may not even hear them, or it could take longer than usual to respond. However, these are all normal cognitive symptoms that can be associated with grieving.

Practicing self-care can help your overwhelmed mind recuperate. This may include making time for healthy eating, sleeping, and exercise. Be intentional about choosing wholesome foods over junk food. Do what you can to promote healthy sleep if your sleep patterns are interrupted, as disrupted sleep can make thinking and concentration difficult. Find ways to move your body. Additionally, you may need time off from work or a break from daily responsibilities to attend to your grief. Prioritize your well-being and make time for healing and self-care.

What are some mental symptoms of grief that you or others
around you have noticed? How are these affecting you?

_____

_____

_____

_____

_____

_____

What steps can you take this week to improve your self-care?
Whom can you ask for help?

_____

_____

_____

_____

_____

_____

_____

_____

Feeling Isolated from Others

In you, Lord my God, I put my trust . . .
Turn to me and be gracious to me, for I am
lonely and afflicted. Relieve the troubles
of my heart and free me from my anguish.

PSALM 25:1, 16–17

It can be unsettling how quickly the world continues to move on after we have experienced the deepest wounds of loss. When we are steeped in the shock of profound change, others around us may not fully understand our need to pause, to get a handle on what is happening. We may choose to withdraw from the company of others who don't get it. Friends may stay distant because they haven't experienced the extent of the grief we are feeling, and they don't know what to do or say. Sometimes our grief stirs up their fears about their own loved ones' mortality, which they may not be ready to face.

Grief can cause us to be preoccupied with our own feelings such that we behave differently. This can change the dynamics of relationships. We may have trouble accepting the different styles of grieving among family members experiencing the same loss. Sometimes it can help to share with friends and family the changes you observe in yourself and your relationships. Invite them to be patient with you to help you get through this time.

In what ways, if any, have you experienced isolation or withdrawal from your family or support community? Make the prayer in Psalm 25 your own today.

....

....

....

....

....

....

....

If you have noticed changes in your relationships, what can you do to let others know how you feel? What investment can you make in relationships that feel distant?

....

....

....

....

....

....

....

....

Tears

Record my misery; list my tears on your scroll—are they not in your record?

PSALM 56:8

Did you know that God records your tears? He sees every tear you shed, and He knows the pain you suffer. God is moved by our tears. In Revelation 21:4, He promises one day to wipe away every tear from our eyes.

When I was grieving several losses that happened within a two-year period, I felt I didn't have time to cry. I was afraid that if I started crying, it would take me hours to stop. A counselor told me that tears provide a release valve for stress-causing chemicals to exit the body. I began to tell myself, "It's okay to cry. It's okay to let yourself feel." What I experienced was that grief came in waves, triggered by a memory, a place, or even an object, like a kitchen utensil. My best cries happened when I cooked food, as I remembered meals I had prepared for my elderly mentor and her husband. When I let the energy of the grief wave take its course, my body relaxed, and I was calm again within minutes. If you have difficulty crying, watching a sad movie or telling your story to an empathetic friend or counselor may help. If you are troubled by how much you are crying, talking to a grief counselor may be your next best step.

What is your relationship with your tears? How easy is it for you to cry? What would help you cry when you need to?

_____

_____

_____

_____

_____

_____

The next time you have the urge to cry, try to let yourself do so. Consider how crying tears of grief can be a healthy way for your body and your mind to collaborate in a time of loss. Try to notice what and how you feel after crying and observe those experiences. Ask yourself what your body and mind are trying to teach you about grieving when they guide you toward release and relief.

_____

_____

_____

_____

_____

_____

Talking to Your Loved One

*Therefore, since we are surrounded
by such a great cloud of witnesses . . .*

HEBREWS 12:1

As Christians we may be reluctant to tell others we talk to our
deceased loved ones. Some may caution us that God doesn't
want us "talking to the dead" or tell us that God desires us to
seek Him alone for guidance. However, as we walk through
grief, that inner conversation with a loved one can be healing.
Grief is often about undelivered communication regarding love,
regrets, guilt, resentment, dreams, and more. We need to speak
for those feelings.

One day I sat in an antique rocking chair that I used to sit in
during conversations with my mentor. With a handmade pillow
from my grandmother's couch, a picture of a recently deceased
friend, and my stepmom's piano in front of me, I gathered my
"moms" in my mind and heart. I told them how much I missed
them and their guidance and prayers. I pondered how they were
joined together in heaven by their common faith and their love
for me. I imagined them telling each other about how special
I was to them. I cried as I thought about these women of faith
being a part of the great cloud of witnesses that surround me.

What would you like to talk about with your loved one(s)?

_____

_____

_____

_____

_____

_____

_____

Picture yourself with them in a comfortable place and tell them what is on your heart. Let your imagination engage with the scene. The way you will know when the Holy Spirit takes over is if your heart feels lighter, or if you imagine something that gives you relief or joy. Reflect on this and write about the imagined encounter.

_____

_____

_____

_____

_____

_____

_____

Observing Grief

Looking Back Exercise:

Review your journal from the past several weeks and notice the various symptoms of grief that you recorded. How have these symptoms changed since your loved one died? How has your physical health been impacted since your loss? Commit to improving your well-being this week by making a conscious decision about what or how much you eat or drink, devoting time to exercise or stretching, or even scheduling a massage to relieve tension.

Take a moment to thank God for the things He has shown you so far and for the ways you are healing. Make a list of the things you are still working on and ask Him to help you with them.

Looking Forward Exercise:

Sometimes during our grief work we find it difficult to process something that happened in our relationship with the person who died. We may be angry at them, or at God, about what transpired. In the next several weeks we will examine feelings grievers often have difficulty processing, such as anger, regret, abandonment, and the feelings associated with unpleasant end-of-life experiences. Use this exercise to acknowledge some of the feelings that need attention.

Sit in a comfortable place with your feet on the floor and take some deep breaths that fully expand your lungs. As you breathe in, acknowledge God's love and His acceptance for how you feel. As you exhale, invite God to carry the burdens you still need to process. Take a moment to acknowledge each difficult or unpleasant feeling you are aware of. The next several weeks will give you an opportunity to reflect on the feelings that present a challenge to your recovery and the antidotes that can lead to healing.

Holy Spirit, please be my Comforter.
Strengthen me, and help me in
this journey. Send the people and
resources that will be a help to me in
the days ahead, in Jesus's name.

Understanding Short-Term Relief

But where sin increased, grace increased all the more.

ROMANS 5:20

Many grieving people turn to short-term relief for the anxiety and other emotions that overwhelm them. Members of one of my grief recovery support groups described it this way: "After my daughter died, I wandered through retail stores buying things I didn't need and hiding the credit card bills from my partner," stated Maria. Darnell had to put down his ill Jack Russell terrier: "The vet wanted $2,000 to do Bolt's surgery. I keep eating junk food to stuff down the guilt I feel about not agreeing to it." Betty described dating again after her spouse died: "At first, all the attention was great," she lamented, "but in six months I slept with five dates. That is not who I want to be."

Short-term relief can be counterproductive, a self-destructive way to cope with grief's inherent intensity; it can take the form of increased drinking, gambling, shopping, eating, overexercising, or other unhealthy habits that we feel shame about. The painful feelings will always return, along with potentially unintended consequences. These behaviors are usually attempts to dull the pain. However, as you process your grief by reflecting on the positives and negatives of your relationship, these behaviors often subside. Support along the way may include talking to a friend or counselor. Find someone who won't judge you or betray your confidence. The tearing of attachment bonds is devastating to the human soul. God is not mad at you. He understands our weaknesses and has abundant grace to help you through this time. There is a path toward healing.

What concerning habits or behaviors have increased or emerged since your loss? How do you feel about them?

What would you like to do differently and why? Who could you talk to about what you are experiencing? Write down a plan to begin to address these issues.

The Truth about Guilt

*If we confess our sins, he is faithful and
just and will forgive us our sins and
purify us from all unrighteousness.*

1 JOHN 1:9

When a client tells me they feel guilty after someone dies, I
don't try to talk them out of it or reassure them that they are not
guilty, because it is important to acknowledge all the feelings
we have while grieving. We first, together, seek to discover the
cause of the guilt. Some people feel guilty because they did or
said something harmful to the person who died. Perhaps it was
an argument or not honoring a loved one's wishes. Others feel
guilty about things when they had no negative intention, such as
how a parent was treated in a nursing home or having to eutha-
nize a suffering pet. Many feel guilty about not visiting enough
or not saying goodbye. Some people feel guilty about difficult
end-of-life decisions. Regardless of the cause of this grief guilt,
there is a remedy. For actual guilt, we confess our sins to the
Lord. For guilt that isn't our fault, we can bring all our burdens
to God and let Him carry them. In either case, the Lord can
show us truth about the situation.

Do you feel responsible for something that didn't go well for your loved one? Take a moment and confess those things to the Lord. As you do, imagine giving each of those weights to Him to carry. Ask the Lord what He wants you to know about each one. Write down the spontaneous thoughts, feelings, or pictures that come to mind.

Are there things that didn't go well for your loved one that were not in your control? Reflect on how it feels to have felt power-less. Give these burdens to the Lord. Ask Him what He wants you to know about each one and write down your impressions.

Validate Your Anger

A bruised reed he will not break, and a
smoldering wick he will not snuff out. In
faithfulness he will bring forth justice.

ISAIAH 42:3

When someone we love dies, we can feel angry about the unfairness of it. The life we expected to enjoy together is gone. Maybe you are angry toward someone you feel let you or your loved one down, such as a doctor, a caregiver, a family member, or even God. Anger is the reaction we feel to a perceived injustice, a thwarted goal, or a disappointed expectation. Anger reminds us that our soul needs attention. Think of anger as trying to protect something valuable to your heart. Though you may feel uncomfortable with anger, especially if you don't understand that it has a good intention for you, God understands you and your anger. Processing anger requires acknowledgment and validation of the sense of injustice or the disappointed dream. When anger is heard and validated, God helps you move into a place of acceptance.

What have you noticed about anger in your heart since your loved one died? How does anger feel in your body? How does anger affect your relationship with God and/or others?

_____

_____

_____

_____

_____

_____

Imagine anger sitting on the floor in front of you. What is anger trying to tell you? What does it want (e.g., "Anger says they didn't give him the right medication" or "Anger wants the life I had before Jody got sick")? Invite Jesus to join your conversation. Picture yourself releasing the burdens of anger to Him one by one. Say, "Lord, I give this to You." Make a list here of the burdens you are releasing.

_____

_____

_____

_____

_____

_____

All Is Not Lost

Now Peter was sitting out in the court-
yard, and a servant girl came to him.
"You also were with Jesus of Galilee," she
said. But he denied it before them all. "I
don't know what you're talking about," he
said . . . Then Peter remembered the word
Jesus had spoken: "Before the rooster
crows, you will disown me three times."
And he went outside and wept bitterly.

MATTHEW 26:69–70, 75

That moment in the courtyard was the last time Peter saw Jesus alive. If only he could take back so hastily denying that he knew Jesus. At this, Peter wept bitterly with regret. After His resurrection, Jesus provided an opportunity for Peter to be restored. In John 21, Jesus met Peter on the shore of the Sea of Galilee for an encounter reminiscent of their first introduction in Luke 5, eventually culminating with a miraculous catch of fish. Jesus knew Peter's regret and sense of hopelessness that what happened could never be fixed. However, Jesus asked Peter to follow Him and to "feed my lambs" and "take care of my sheep" (John 21:15–16). Jesus let Peter know that in spite of his moment of failure in their relationship, all was not lost.

Do you need a restorative moment with your loved one? Ask the Lord to take you back to the place you wish you had done or said something differently. Picture your loved one in the scene. Take the opportunity to make an apology or ask for forgiveness. Say what you didn't get to say before. Write down your reflections.

....

....

....

....

....

....

Ask Jesus to show you how your loved one would respond to the things you say. Tune in to the flow of spontaneous thoughts, feelings, impressions, and pictures. Write down what comes to mind without judgment. When you finish writing, read what you wrote. How does it make you feel?

....

....

....

....

....

Peace after Trauma

The Lord is close to the brokenhearted
and saves those who are crushed in spirit.

PSALM 34:18

If something traumatic happened shortly before your loved one died, troubling images and thoughts may hijack positive memories. To mourn effectively and healthily, we need to remember, but if remembering becomes painful, we avoid it. Confronting and resolving these disturbing memories will help you move forward.

At Alena's first counseling appointment with me, she described crying every day since her mother died two years ago. She recalled leaving the nursing home briefly to retrieve things from home. While away, the staff tried to get her near-comatose mother out of bed. She fell and died two days later. Alena was racked with guilt: "If I hadn't left, this wouldn't have happened." As an exercise, Alena conversed with her "younger self" from two years ago, acknowledging and validating her decisions and how awful the outcome was. Alena was able to tell herself that she was not to blame, and she chose to forgive the nursing home staff. When she returned the next week, Alena smiled. "When I drive by the nursing home, I don't feel distressed anymore. I know my mom is at peace and she is not mad at me."

Loss can be traumatic. Sometimes, we get stuck in bad memories or feelings of guilt associated with a loved one's death. Have a compassionate dialogue with the part of you that relives those moments. Acknowledge and validate those feelings (e.g., "It makes sense to me why you would be upset about that"). Continue a loving and supportive conversation, reassuring your past self that you did the best you could under the circumstances surrounding your loss. Write down your reflections.

Invite Jesus to show you where He was and what He was doing in the troubling scenes. Use your imagination to sense Him showing you. Write down any changes to how you feel. If end-of-life memories of your loved one continue to bother you, please seek out a trained professional for help.

Saying Goodbye to Their Physical Presence

So with you: Now is your time of grief, but
I will see you again and you will rejoice,
and no one will take away your joy.

JOHN 16:22

When Jesus told His disciples that they would grieve His absence, they had no idea He would die such a traumatic death. Most of the disciples went into hiding and were not present at the cross. Surely they carried a heavy burden for not being able to say goodbye to their beloved rabbi. They were fortunate not to have to carry their grief beyond three days, when Jesus rose from the grave.

Many of us wish for such an encounter with loved ones, where three days after their deaths we could meet again, share a meal, and embrace one more time. Although the disciples got a marvelous glimpse into the meaning of resurrection, Jesus still physically left them 40 days later when He ascended. They still had to live life without Jesus's physical presence. They had to say goodbye to their physical relationship with Him and transition to a relationship facilitated by the Holy Spirit, who was promised to live in them, remind them of what Jesus said, and empower them to carry on His ministry by sharing the Gospel throughout the world. Like the disciples, we also need to transition to a different kind of relationship with our loved ones. We need to say goodbye to our physical relationship while holding the memory of our love and experience with them in our hearts.

Take time to remember moments of being in the bodily presence of your loved one, and hold in your mind what it felt like to be with them in person. What do you cherish most about your time together, your physical relationship? What do you miss most about being with them, in their presence? What is the most difficult part about this for you?

_____

_____

_____

_____

_____

_____

_____

When you think of resurrection for you or your loved one, what do you imagine it will be like?

_____

_____

_____

_____

_____

_____

Identity

"Don't call me Naomi," she told them. "Call me Mara, because the Almighty has made my life very bitter."

RUTH 1:20

Naomi's grief chafed against her name after the deaths of her husband and two sons. Her name means *pleasant*. In grief she said she should be called "Mara," which means *bitter* in Hebrew.

Life after loss can mean having to accept a new sense of self. The death of a spouse means you are a widow or widower instead of a partner. The death of a parent can arouse feelings of loneliness and disconnection, since our parents often shape our relationship to life and self. When we lose a friend, a pet, or a mentor, part of us changes. Acceptance of a new identity can be one of the most challenging aspects of grief. This new identity may manifest in uncomfortable ways, such as while filling out forms asking for marital status, finding yourself sitting alone at church or social functions, or feeling the sting of absence around a holiday dinner table.

While the Bible doesn't indicate that Naomi was ever a wife or parent again, her story did take a positive turn when her daughter-in-law, Ruth, married Boaz and produced a grand-child. "Then Naomi took the child in her arms and cared for him. The women living there said, 'Naomi has a son!' And they named him Obed. He was the father of Jesse, the father of David" (Ruth 4:16–17). Not only did Naomi become a grand-mother, but through her tragedy, eventually Jesus came as the son of David through her lineage. In loss, there is also opportunity to know ourselves differently and to grow in that knowledge.

In what ways has your identity changed since your loss? Consider what has been lost and what has been gained.

_____

_____

_____

_____

_____

_____

_____

If God "is able to do immeasurably more than all we ask or imagine" (Ephesians 3:20), what could you imagine God doing to bring blessing, healing, and redemption to your story of loss?

_____

_____

_____

_____

_____

_____

Abandonment

Be strong and courageous. Do not be afraid or terrified because of them, for the Lord your God goes with you; he will never leave you nor forsake you.

When we lose someone we depend on, it is natural to feel abandoned. Feelings of abandonment highlight our desire for our loved one to need or help us, to advise or encourage us. It may be a struggle to do things on your own that your loved one used to do. You may have even experienced abandonment by people who are living who have not come through for you the way you needed them to during this time.

In whatever abandonment you have experienced, remember that God is Immanuel, God with us. He will never leave you. It may feel strange at first, but you can train yourself to turn to God for the things you depended on others for. If you need a hug, help with household chores, or social interaction, let God know, and let Him figure out how to bring you what you need. He "is able to do immeasurably more than all we ask or imagine" (Ephesians 3:20). Ask and watch what happens.

In what ways do you feel abandoned? Who can you turn to for help? If you don't have any immediate friends or family in your life right now, consider looking into a counselor, support group, or church organization to make new connections.

_____

_____

_____

_____

_____

_____

What are your needs when you feel abandoned? Pray and ask the Lord to surprise you with His grace, even if you have trouble believing that He could answer your prayer.

_____

_____

_____

_____

_____

_____

_____

Saying Goodbye

When Paul had finished speaking . . .
They all wept as they embraced him
and kissed him. What grieved them
most was his statement that they
would never see his face again.

ACTS 20:36–38

My mentor's health was precarious for several years due to
congestive heart failure. Many times, Hazel's family gathered
around her hospital bed believing she would die soon. Several
years later, she had hospice care at home. I stopped in to see
her and said goodbye one last time before returning to graduate
school two hours away. Hazel passed away in the middle of the
night, as witnessed by her son, who described sensing the presence of angels and supernatural peace as she entered eternity.

Most of us imagine that when the time comes for a loved
one to transition from this life, we will have time to say all we
need to. However, tragic accidents, suicide, travel restrictions,
complicated relationships, hospital or nursing home rules, etc.,
can hinder our ability to say an adequate goodbye. Without a
sense of completion in saying goodbye, the feelings won't fade
on their own. Finding a creative way to finish the unfinished
business will lead to a greater sense of wholeness and help us
come to terms with our losses.

If you had the opportunity to say goodbye to your loved one before they passed, write about your experience here.

....

....

....

....

....

....

....

If you did not get to say all that was on your heart, take time to do that now. Picture yourself with your loved one. Invite Jesus to join you. Express your love and/or regrets. Write down your reflections.

....

....

....

....

....

....

....

....

Grief Is for a Season

*Weeping may stay for the night, but
rejoicing comes in the morning.*

PSALM 30:5

The change and separation that come from loss are devastating. Loss reduces familiar patterns of life to memories of the past. Some losses we never *get over*, but with time and the right attention, we do integrate them into our lives so that we can experience joy and pleasure again. Grief is a season in life that almost no one escapes, but it doesn't last forever. Have you had other losses in the past? Maybe as a child your grandparents or other relatives died, or perhaps you went through your parents' divorce. You may have experienced losing a pet, moving, or changing schools. Later there may have been the breakup of a romantic relationship or the loss of a job. Grief is cumulative, and whatever losses you didn't fully process in the past will likely show up again as you mourn today. Be gentle with and pay attention to those feelings; they are letting you know what still needs to be addressed. It's okay if you're not "over it." When those feelings come up, it is an invitation to move toward healing.

Reflect on previous losses you have experienced over your life. How did you recover a sense of normalcy in life again? Which losses continue to impact you today? If past losses continue to hinder your ability to heal, it may be time to talk to a grief counselor for help.

....

....

....

....

....

How do you imagine your life after loss, after a season of grief? What do you imagine as your season of renewal? Write down your reflections, hopes, or doubts about the potential joyous future described in the verse above.

....

....

....

....

....

....

Observing Grief

Looking Back Exercise:

Do you talk to yourself? The Bible has several examples of people talking to their own soul, reminding themselves of God's love, His faithfulness, and what He has done in the past (e.g., Psalm 42:5, 103:1–2, 116:7; Jeremiah 4:19; Judges 5:21).

Take a walk or sit in a comfortable chair, and picture any distressing feelings as if they were standing around you or walking with you. Thank each one for holding something important for you to process. Have a compassionate conversation with each one that starts something like this:

"Anger, thank you for letting me know that there was something that offended me or that felt unjust . . ."

"Regret, I know you feel bad about what happened. Is there something you want to apologize for?"

"Fear, I know there are a lot of unknowns right now. Let me remind you about how God took care of my needs in the past . . ."

"Grief, I get it that it feels bad. I will get through this."

Validate each feeling with a phrase like, "It makes sense to me that you would feel that way." Remember past times when you have faced uncomfortable feelings and how God helped you make it through.

Write a prayer thanking God for any burdens that feel lighter. Thank the Lord that He has a plan for your future.

Looking Forward Exercise:

Imagine that you are in a place in the future when you have more adequately adjusted to living without your loved one and you have more peace in your life. What would you be doing differently? What is one step you can take this week to help you move closer to that vision? After you take that step, do something to reward yourself.

Father God, I ask You to fill my heart with courage and a vision for what You have for my future. Please give me hope in Your plans and purpose for my life, in Jesus's name.

Finding Community

Perfume and incense bring joy to
the heart, and the pleasantness of a
friend springs from their heartfelt advice.

PROVERBS 27:9

Usually, supportive people are available at the time of your loss. Yet, grief has a way of weighing down your relationships. The weeks and months that follow a loss can feel isolating. You may believe that others don't understand what you are going through. If your social group was mostly couples and now you are widowed, it can be hard to stay connected. Likewise, if you have lost a pet, your friends may not realize how deeply you are grieving. A grief support group may be helpful, joining with others to better understand the grief experience. However, after a while you may want to reengage with life's activities outside of grief. If it feels awkward to participate in the community you were previously a part of, it may be time to look for new groups. Where can you find these groups? Try churches, clubs for specific hobbies like art or music or tennis, a community center, a Meetup group, a singles' group, or a neighborhood group. Volunteering or a new job might also be a path toward renewal and possibility. Online groups may help you fill a need for connection without even having to leave home.

What kinds of groups and activities are you interested in?
Where have you met people and felt connected in the past?
Make a list of ideas of where you might find a new community or
restore yourself to a previous one.

It may be difficult or scary to go places to meet new people
when you feel vulnerable. Spend some time praying and asking
the Lord for guidance and direction. He knows where your new
friends are. Write your prayer and reflections.

The God of the Living

But in the account of the burning bush, even Moses showed that the dead rise, for he calls the Lord "the God of Abraham, and the God of Isaac, and the God of Jacob." He is not the God of the dead, but of the living, for to him all are alive.

LUKE 20:37–38

We think of death differently than God does. We think of death as being an end: an end of life on earth as we know it. An end of a relationship. For many of us, death feels like a permanent change. To God, however, death is a transition "away from the body and at home with the Lord" (2 Corinthians 5:8). When Jesus prays for His disciples and all who will believe because of their message, He states, "Now this is eternal life: that they know you, the only true God, and Jesus Christ, whom you have sent" (John 17:3). He indicates that eternal life doesn't start when we die but when we know God through Jesus Christ. When I experienced the loss of several people close to me, I found it helpful to read books about what the Bible says about heaven. These books encouraged me to contemplate the wonderful life my loved ones were experiencing at any moment I thought about them. Some of these titles can be found in the Resources section at the end of the book (page 119).

What does the phrase *God of the living* mean to you? Do you struggle with the concept of eternal life in heaven? What would you ask God about life after death if you had the chance? Write down your reflections.

_____

_____

_____

_____

_____

_____

What is it like to think of your loved one as living in heaven? Who have they reunited with? What do you imagine them doing?

_____

_____

_____

_____

_____

_____

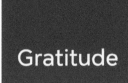

Gratitude

*Rejoice always, pray continually, give
thanks in all circumstances; for this
is God's will for you in Christ Jesus.*

1 THESSALONIANS 5:16–18

How can you give thanks in painful circumstances? At the Last
Supper, Jesus "took bread, gave thanks and broke it, and gave
it to them" (Luke 22:19). Jesus gave thanks while considering
His own impending death. Hebrews 12:2 says, "For the joy set
before him he endured the cross." He could give thanks looking forward to the redemption that would allow people to be
restored to fellowship with Him.

Giving thanks in grief can be an act of faith. It could include
thanking God for the positive influence your loved one had in
your life and for the experiences you shared. Gratitude may
be simpler, noting that you have food, shelter, and friends
and family who care about you. You can give thanks for small
moments of beauty such as the sound of a child's laughter, the
scent of a flower, or the taste of ripe fruit.

Researchers of positive psychology have found that writing
down gratitude statements can release toxic emotions, improve
the ability to handle stress, and reduce symptoms of anxiety
and depression. An attitude of gratitude can even reduce pain
and improve sleep. Subjects in the studies wrote gratitude
journals or thank-you notes and offered verbal expressions of
appreciation.

Which ways of expressing gratitude appeal to you? What will you do to make this a more regular habit in your life?

_____

_____

_____

_____

_____

_____

Begin a list here: Who can you thank? What are you thankful for?

_____

_____

_____

_____

_____

_____

_____

_____

Peace and Grace during Trials

May God himself, the God of peace,
sanctify you through and through. May
your whole spirit, soul and body be kept
blameless at the coming of our Lord
Jesus Christ. The one who calls you is
faithful, and he will do it . . . The grace
of our Lord Jesus Christ be with you.

1 THESSALONIANS 5:23–24, 28

The apostle Paul wrote this letter to the church in Thessalonica to encourage the Thessalonians who were suffering hardship and persecution for their faith. These believers likely were experiencing grief due to changes they didn't have control over when their property was seized, they lost their jobs, or they were shunned by family members for their beliefs. They may have even grieved for fellow believers who were executed for their faith. Amid difficult circumstances Paul prayed for the "God of peace" to minister to them and help them live in a blameless way. Perhaps you need the God of peace to calm your anxiety or to help you feel less irritable about changes you don't have control over. Walking out our faith with grace and peace during times of pain and distress is a supernatural endeavor. Invite the God of peace to sanctify you: "He is faithful, and He will do it."

How has God shown you His peace or grace in this season? In what ways are you struggling through the trials and in need of encouragement?

_____

_____

_____

_____

_____

_____

In what areas do you need more peace or grace at this time? How would focusing on the coming of the Lord Jesus Christ affect how you live today?

_____

_____

_____

_____

_____

_____

_____

Hope

*Brothers and sisters, we do not want
you to be uninformed about those who
sleep in death, so that you do not grieve
like the rest of mankind, who have no
hope. For we believe that Jesus died and
rose again, and so we believe that God
will bring with Jesus those who have
fallen asleep in him ... Therefore
encourage one another with these words.*

1 THESSALONIANS 4:13–14, 18

We can meditate on and imagine what the experience of heaven
is like for our loved ones. When we do, we find there is hope and
healing in surrendering to the thought that peace is possible for
those we have loved, as well as for ourselves. God's Word tells
us to "set your hearts on things above" (Colossians 3:1). He provides images in scripture to describe heaven because He wants
us to contemplate our future beyond our time on earth. We don't
grieve as those who have no hope. We are to encourage one
another with the words of this passage, using our imagination to
picture the dead in Christ rising.

Sometimes we grieve with distress because we are unsure of the condition of someone's heart when they died. Are they in heaven? Perhaps the way they lived their life suggests they didn't want anything to do with God. Have a conversation with God about your concerns about your loved one's place in eternity and reflect on those insights here.

....

....

....

....

....

Even while we do not understand all of God's ways, we know He is merciful. According to Revelation 21:4, God has a plan to wipe away every tear from our eyes. How does the Word of God offer you hope in your grief?

....

....

....

....

....

....

God's Voice

My sheep listen to my voice; I know them,
and they follow me. I give them eternal
life, and they shall never perish; no
one will snatch them out of my hand.

JOHN 10:27–28

God's voice is a promise to every believer, but not every believer recognizes God's voice. I learned from books by Mark Virkler how to quiet my mind and heart, fix my eyes on Jesus, ask God questions, and then pay attention to the spontaneous flow of thoughts, impressions, feelings, and pictures that came to mind and write them down. Not everything came from God, but to encourage my soul I could review my journal to see what lined up with the Word of God and with God's heart. I shared life-altering ideas with my mentors to help me sort out God's plan for my life and ministry. Working in church ministry, and then as a therapist, I have helped others hear God's voice as well. Many times, people knew they had sensed guidance as an inner knowledge of the right thing to do, or they felt comforted after praying, but they didn't realize that was how God was speaking to them. Other people had encouraging thoughts or a scripture verse come to mind to interrupt their negative thinking or feelings. Sometimes a friend offered helpful advice just when they needed it. When we understand how God speaks, we can look forward to tuning in to His voice daily for fellowship, healing, support, and guidance.

In what ways have you been aware of God speaking to you? What do you sense that He is saying now?

_____

_____

_____

_____

_____

_____

Sometimes when we go through hard times, we lose our sense of where God is. If you are finding it difficult to hear God (or if you have never been sure that you are hearing His voice), what steps would you be willing to take to address this?

_____

_____

_____

_____

_____

_____

_____

Quiet Your Heart

Be still, and know that I am God; I
will be exalted among the nations, I
will be exalted in the earth.

PSALM 46:10

Quieting our hearts in a distracting world is a challenge. When I intend to be quiet, my electronic devices can interrupt, or my mind serves up a to-do list. While grieving, when I became still, unpleasant emotions surfaced. When they did, a part of me suggested snacks, social media updates, or other diversions. When quiet time competes with busy work schedules and other responsibilities, it can be frustrating. It is especially challenging when daily life leaves no room for being with ourselves quietly and purposefully. But it is important to find ways to be present in our grief and to feel what we feel without distracting ourselves or diverting our pain.

For seasons in my life, especially when grieving, sometimes I gave up trying to have quiet time with God. Sometimes I felt too angry or it was too painful. I found other ways to let God in because I knew I needed His help. I read books by authors who struggled through parts of life they didn't understand. I listened to worship music to help lift my attitude toward God. By faith, I worshiped God even when I didn't feel like it. For me the books were most helpful because I've been mentored by books throughout my life. Eventually, I came to some acceptance of the losses and felt on more friendly terms with God again. It became easier to become still and acknowledge that no matter what, God is who He says He is, and I can trust Him.

What distractions do you notice when you try to quiet your heart to have time with God? What strategies could help you overcome the distractions? Have you tried any?

....

....

....

....

....

....

What feelings do you notice come up for you when you are still? Acknowledge each of your feelings and write about them.

....

....

....

....

....

....

....

Fix Your Eyes on Jesus

And let us run with perseverance the race marked out for us, fixing our eyes on Jesus, the pioneer and perfecter of faith.

HEBREWS 12:1–2

When we are confused, fearful, unsure, worried, and in need of guidance, fixing the eyes of our heart on Jesus is always the next best step. In turning toward God, we turn toward perseverance and realize we are not alone. We can use our imagination to picture Jesus with us in our situation. This is how we run with perseverance the path before us even when we are tired and uncertain. We acknowledge the Lord's presence and seek His help and direction. What would Jesus do in this situation? What would He want us to know about our situation? In my experience of listening for and teaching others to hear God's voice, I've noticed that He doesn't always directly answer what I am asking when I am asking it, but He provides a flow of comforting thoughts and/or scriptures that reassure me that I belong to Him, that He cares about my concern, and that He is working on my behalf.

When you fix your eyes on Jesus, how do you picture Him with you? Write down what you see or sense.

What areas of your life would it be helpful to talk to God about? Spend some time sharing these areas with the Lord and ask what He is saying about them. Write down the spontaneous thoughts that come to mind. Review these words and ask yourself, do they sound like something God would say to you?

Express Your Evolving Thoughts

This is what the Lord, the God of Israel, says: "Write in a book all the words I have spoken to you."

JEREMIAH 30:2

Biblical prophets and psalmists recorded their prayers, praises, and emotions. Neuroscientists have found that writing down our feelings is a healthy habit. Journaling can reduce the intensity of pain, sadness, anxiety, and anger. Journaling can help you release preoccupying thoughts or to-do lists and help you fall asleep. When you write something down, your brain relaxes.

Another form of journaling is prayer, when we ask God questions and then pay attention to the spontaneous thoughts, words, impressions, and pictures that come to mind and write them down. When we write down what we sense God is saying, it doesn't always mean that we have heard accurately. Where there is guidance, and especially before making major life changes, it is wise to share your journaling with trusted advisers who know you and who also know how to hear God's voice. Their wisdom can protect you from making big mistakes.

A journal can take many forms, including lists or writing about memories, emotions, or plans. You can also write letters to yourself or others to help you process events or feelings. Writing letters to your loved one can help you express things left unsaid at the time of their passing, or it can be a way to express your evolving thoughts and attitudes about life since then.

Set aside time to write down some of your thoughts relating to grief and your life after loss, as well as your fears and your uncertainties. Allow yourself to write freely without overthinking. Perhaps start by making a list of how your life seems to have changed.

If you have been reluctant to journal in the past, what are you hesitant about? Privacy? Not knowing what to write? The Resources section at the end of this book provides some options (page 119). There are also resources available online. Make some notes here about possible solutions to these difficulties.

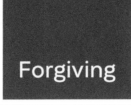

Forgiving

*Bear with each other and
forgive one another if any of you
has a grievance against someone.
Forgive as the Lord forgave you.*

COLOSSIANS 3:13

When we have been hurt by someone, it can be hard to let go of the anger. Anger feels even more difficult to let go if the one who offended us is no longer alive to discuss it. Until we make peace with the past and release the offense, we risk being triggered every time we think of the person. This can make grieving more difficult and last longer. We can choose to forgive. We do not need an apology from anyone. Forgiveness means to release a debt. When we forgive, we are releasing the emotional debt that is owed us because of another person's actions. It is accepting the consequences of someone else's sin or choice. You are living with the consequences. When you choose to accept the consequences you are already living with, you create a peaceful path for your heart.

What offenses are you holding on to from someone who has passed away? Which ones would you be willing to release for your healing?

....

....

....

....

....

....

This is a brief statement or prayer that I use with my clients to help them release resentment and unforgiveness: "I choose to forgive _____ (name) for _____ (specifically what they did that hurt you), which made me feel _____ (the emotional debt they owe). I release the debt they owe me." Write down your reflections. What difference does it make for you as you release these things?

....

....

....

....

....

....

Compassion

For no one is cast off by the Lord forever. Though he brings grief, he will show compassion, so great is his unfailing love. For he does not willingly bring affliction or grief to anyone.

LAMENTATIONS 3:31–33

When we suffer a devastating loss, it can be hard to believe that God is compassionate or loving. No matter how hard it may be to accept that a loving God would allow your loved one to suffer or die, He loves you and cares for you, and He "does not willingly bring affliction or grief to anyone." For millennia God has heard from the depths of human hearts how they disagree or disapprove of His plans, His ways, or His timing. Sometimes we get indignant when the pain of suffering and loss touches our lives and we aren't prepared for it. God has big shoulders and can handle you expressing your anger, confusion, or doubt about what has happened and how it affects your view of His character. Pour your heart out to Him. Tell him how you really feel. He wants to reveal His compassion to you and mend your broken heart. His heart breaks as well, because His original intention was for people to live forever and never experience the separation of death.

What do you need to tell God right now, in this moment? What would you want Him to know?

In what ways do you need God's compassion revealed to you today? In what ways have you experienced His compassion recently? Write about your reflections.

Comfort in His Blessings

Though you have made me see troubles,
many and bitter, you will restore my life
again; from the depths of the earth you
will again bring me up. You will increase
my honor and comfort me once more.

PSALM 71:20–21

The psalmist writes with hope that his situation in life will change after experiencing "troubles, many and bitter." Consider the history of your life, or the lives of others in the generation before you. Can you think of examples of times of difficulty that eventually resolved to bring honor and comfort? I think of friends who have found love again after being widowed or divorced, and clients who've had miscarriages but eventually gave birth or adopted children to create a family. I know people who lost their houses to foreclosure and then were able to move to another home. Some went through an anxious time of unemployment before being hired at a place they now love to work.

It may be hard to imagine a time in the future when you feel peace and contentment. In fact, it may feel disloyal to your loved one to contemplate it. Grief complicates our desire for comfort and can obscure our ability to see the blessings that might arise out of loss. Nevertheless, God has a habit of bringing blessing out of chaos and disappointment. My sister was pregnant with the first grandchild in the family when our stepmom died. As one family member was leaving, a new one joined us two months later. We are disappointed they didn't get to meet their grandmother, but today there are five grandchildren who bring great joy to the family.

What are some examples in your life of painful circumstances being resolved into blessing?

_____

_____

_____

_____

_____

_____

_____

What examples do you have from the lives of people you know who have experienced restoration and comfort after loss?

_____

_____

_____

_____

_____

_____

_____

Observing Grief

Looking Back Exercise:

Take a walk or drive to a place that is significant in your memory of your loved one. It could be a place you visited together in the past or the cemetery where they are buried. Find a peaceful place with a nature view, if possible. As you observe and absorb your surroundings, take some deep breaths, filling your lungs, and then exhale to release tension from your body. Notice and appreciate the beauty of the season around you. If you have a sense of your loved one's presence, share with them what's on your heart. Consider your relationship with God. Do you sense His presence near to you or far away? What do you think He wants you to know today?

Write a prayer thanking God for His help during your season of loss. Talk to Him about your relationship with your loved one today and how you feel about it, as well as where you would like it to be.

....

....

....

....

....

....

Looking Forward Exercise:

As you look to the future, what would help you grow spiritually? Would it be a renewed commitment to worship, reading the Word, or prayer? Consider joining a group for Bible study and fellowship at your church. Alternatively, there are several community organizations where people gather from different churches, such as Bible Study Fellowship, Precept Bible Study, International Christian Women's Club, Aglow International, and Full Gospel Business Men's Fellowship. Using your gifts to serve others can also help you grow spiritually. Consider volunteering with a church or community organization. Take a step forward this week to find a new place to learn, serve, and grow.

Lord Jesus, You know where I am today in my spiritual walk. You know how this grief has affected my faith, my relationship with You and with others. I put it all in Your hands. I ask You to renew my spirit with Your love and fill me with anticipation for Your plans and purposes in my life, in Your name.

Celebrate the Individual

*Your teeth are like a flock of sheep just
shorn, coming up from the washing. Each
has its twin; not one of them is alone . . .
Your neck is like an ivory tower. Your eyes
are the pools of Heshbon by the gate of
Bath Rabbim. Your nose is like the tower
of Lebanon looking toward Damascus.*

SONG OF SOLOMON 4:2, 7:4

I find humor in these verses as Solomon describes his bride's
smile with attention to the fact that she has all her teeth. This is
an example of recognizing and celebrating a loved one's indi-
viduality and presence in your life. Each person has endearing
personal characteristics that become familiar to us over the
years. It could be the color of their eyes, the way they walk, the
way they wear their hair, the location of their freckles or moles,
the size of their hands, the sound of their voice, and innumer-
able other features that make them unique. I remember the
sparkle in my mentor's eyes when she smiled and the sound of
her laughter. Strangers always commented on the flamboyant
hats my grandma created and wore for holidays and special
occasions. When one is in a state of grief over the loss of a loved
one, there can be something powerful in remembering and celebrating their distinctive traits, physical and otherwise.

What are some unique characteristics about your loved one? What features were special to you? If nothing immediately comes to mind, look through photos or videos that include your loved one. What characteristics do you notice or remember?

What features of your loved one do you miss the most? Think about the first time you noticed them. Record your reflections.

An Antidote for Grief

Even in laughter the heart may ache,
and rejoicing may end in grief.

PROVERBS 14:13

My family has always enjoyed words and puns. At the restaurant for lunch after my stepmom's funeral, I was sitting next to my dad when a friend asked where Mom would be buried. I overheard my dad respond that she would be cremated and that he called to get information on the *columbarium*. It was a word I never heard before. With a puzzled look I asked him, "Call and bury 'em?" Later, I told him I found a number for a discount service called Eucarium Ubarium.

Another story we enjoy recalling in my family is when Mom set the oven on fire with Toll House Cookie Pie. Apparently, the pie pans were a tad too small, and the sugary goodness boiled over and caught fire in the oven. It took a long time to get that burnt smell out of the house.

Humor can be an antidote to grief. Telling funny stories involving lost loved ones, whether significant or mundane, in a way brings them closer to us and restores their presence in our lives. It may only be those who remember who enjoy the stories, but tell them anyway . . . for yourself and for the memory of your loved ones.

What are some funny things that happened to or with your loved one? What are funny stories that were told by friends and family about them?

....

....

....

....

....

....

Are there humorous things that have happened since they've gone that you wish you could tell them about? Write a note to your loved one sharing about these events.

....

....

....

....

....

....

....

A Familiar Scent

So he went to him and kissed him.
When Isaac caught the smell of his
clothes, he blessed him and said, "Ah,
the smell of my son is like the smell of
a field that the Lord has blessed."

GENESIS 27:27

Widows and widowers, as well as those who have lost a child or a pet, have told me that one of the things they miss about their loved one is their smell. Some hold on to clothing that was worn by their loved one before they died, to retain a hint of that unique scent. Sometimes going into your loved one's home brings back memories because of familiar odors.

At my grandma's home, the day after she died, I found a bottle of perfume in the bathroom that reminded me of her scent. My aunt told me that Grandpa used to bring back this perfume from Japan when he was traveling with the Merchant Marines. It had never occurred to me that Grandma was wearing perfume, but the smell from this bottle smelled just like her. I now have it on my dresser where I can inhale the scent every so often when I want to remember her presence again.

What do you remember about your loved one's scent? When do you miss their unique fragrance? What other smells remind you of your loved one?

_____

_____

_____

_____

_____

_____

_____

How would you describe your loved one's scent? Do you remember the smell of perfume/cologne, the smell of cooking in their home, or another smell from their home? What ways, if any, do you recapture your experience of this scent?

_____

_____

_____

_____

_____

_____

The Laughter and the Dancing

A time to be born and a time to die…
a time to weep and a time to laugh, a
time to mourn and a time to dance.

ECCLESIASTES 3:2,4

Fun can seem inappropriate when we are grieving a loved one. Laughing may feel disrespectful. To allow pleasure in your life again might suggest that you are "getting over" their death too soon or betraying your loved one by "forgetting" your grief. Sometimes we fear the judgment of others who might imply we are not mourning enough for someone we loved. It is easy to think about the fun we had before they died, because those memories warm our hearts as we grieve for the special times in the past. After a loss, it may even be difficult to imagine being happy again. However, in today's scripture verse, notice the order. First birth, then death; weeping is followed by laughter; mourning, then dancing. This passage brings a hopeful revelation that the laughter and dancing come after the weeping and mourning. As we reflect on positive memories from the past, keep in mind that even after a devastating loss, your story is not finished, nor is your capacity for joy. Deciding to make time for pleasure and fun is not to leave behind your sense of loss; it is a way to honor life. To restore your capacity for enjoyment is to participate in the cycles of mourning and living the passage above describes.

When you think of fun, what memories come to mind with your loved one? Write about two or three events, including what happened and how you felt at the time.

....

....

....

....

....

....

Fun helps us relax during stress and improves quality of life. In what ways can you allow yourself pleasure in your life today? It might not be the way it used to be, but how can you allow yourself a pathway toward enjoyment again?

....

....

....

....

....

....

....

Intimacy

*Isaac brought her into the tent
of his mother Sarah, and he married
Rebekah. So she became his wife,
and he loved her; and Isaac was
comforted after his mother's death.*

GENESIS 24:67

Three days after their two-year-old drowned in the neighbor's pool, Carol's husband was approaching her to be intimate. Carol was offended. "How could he want sex at a time like this? Our baby just died." Dan felt embarrassed and confused. He asked me for help because Carol wouldn't talk to him. He felt isolated. Dan commented, "I just wanted to connect with her, but there is this huge wall between us. We will always have this grief. Will we never be intimate again?"

Most people find sex soothing and pleasurable. However, when we grieve, we may feel guilty about having pleasure, as if we are betraying the memory of the person who died. But life continues after loss. There will be times of sadness. There will be times of joy again. At some point you will be able to return to enjoyable activities again. Until then, try to communicate openly and honestly with your partner, and share with them your needs and expectations, perhaps saying something like this: "I want to be close to you and affectionate, but I am not yet ready for sex. I will let you know when I'm ready."

If your partner has passed away, you may long for the intimacy you once had. Some describe this as a physical ache to be touched and held again. The longing for touch and affection may be partially soothed in a variety of ways, such as making an appointment for a massage, shaking hands, or hugging friends and relatives. If you feel ready for service opportunities, you might consider caring for babies in the church nursery or volunteering as a baby cuddler in the NICU at your local hospital.

In what ways do you communicate about your need for touch and affection?

....

....

....

....

....

....

What are your thoughts and feelings about sex and intimacy as you deal with loss? Write your reflections here.

....

....

....

....

....

....

God's Purpose Fulfilled

Now when David had served God's purpose in his own generation, he fell asleep; he was buried with his ancestors and his body decayed.

ACTS 13:36

We may agree in principle that everyone will eventually die, but as we are living life, we usually don't spend time dwelling on the fact that those we love and care for are included in this reality. When the death of a family member, friend, or pet touches us, we can be surprised by how deeply we feel the pain. God's Word tells us in Psalm 139 "all the days ordained for me were written in your book before one of them came to be" (verse 16). We celebrate days when we and our loved ones came into the world, but then we want to ignore our expiration dates. Yet, one day, when we have served God's purpose in our generation, it will be time for all of us to die. This week we reflect on the ways that our loved ones served God's purpose in their generation.

God's purpose can be fulfilled through a spouse, parent, sibling, friend, pet, teacher, child, etc. It can also be fulfilled by completing an assignment such as writing a book, working in one's profession, carrying a responsibility to effect change, or participating in some form of leadership.

Make a list of thoughts about how you saw God's purposes fulfilled in your loved one's life. Are there positive things that have happened since they died, related to their life? Write about those here.

What did your loved one accomplish? What made their life meaningful? What legacy remains of your loved one's life and how does that legacy affect or shape your own life in positive ways? Record your reflections.

Talents

*Each of you should use
whatever gift you have received to
serve others, as faithful stewards of
God's grace in its various forms.*

1 PETER 4:10

Our gifts and talents allow us to express beauty and compassion to the world. What were the gifts and talents of your loved one? I am thankful for my music teacher stepmom, who got me started with piano and violin lessons when I was young. My mentor and my grandmother both had the gift of evangelism and regularly started conversations with strangers about Jesus. My friend Lois was wise and always guarded confidences. My great-uncle John was a Sunday school teacher for four-year olds for 40 years. Darelyn was a friend and partner in ministry, as well as a prayer warrior who loved to share fresh-baked chocolate chip cookies. Some of them lived to advanced years. Others seemed to me too young to be finished with this life. All of them finished their race and went home to be with Jesus, but not before leaving their mark of love on hundreds, if not thousands, of lives in their homes, neighborhoods, and ministries, including mine.

Did your loved one have a special talent or ability? Cooking? Fixing things? Art, music, teaching, serving, speaking? Reflect on how you saw these talents operate in their life.

_____

_____

_____

_____

_____

_____

How were your loved one's talents a blessing to you? In what ways do you want to be like them? What did you learn from watching their life? Write down your reflections.

_____

_____

_____

_____

_____

_____

_____

Gifts and Presents

Then they opened their treasures
and presented him with gifts of
gold, frankincense and myrrh.
MATTHEW 2:11

Many people give gifts for birthdays, anniversaries, holidays, and other special occasions. Sometimes people give gifts for no special reason other than to express a form of love. Do you have a history of giving and receiving gifts with your loved one? It is likely there are particular gifts given to you by your loved one that you cherish and will always keep.

I have a collectible figurine of an angel holding a house that my mentor gave me years ago, at a time when I was worried about where I would live. She told me she was praying that God would provide me a home. Today the angel sits on a prominent shelf in the home I could only have dreamed of at the time, reminding me of that prayer that God answered.

My neighbor Eddie recalls the bittersweet day his father gave him his toolbox: "I was in awe that he always had just the right tool needed for every project. But I knew as he gave the tools to me, he was telling me he would be dying soon and would no longer need them. Whenever I use them, I think of watching him use the tools or showing me how to use them when I was a boy. Those are good memories."

What gifts did you give to your loved one? How did they respond? How did you feel about acquiring, creating, and/or presenting these gifts? Write your reflections.

....

....

....

....

....

....

....

What gifts did you receive from your loved one that created special memories? Some gifts may come after a death, such as a piece of jewelry or other inheritance. How did you feel or how do you feel now about gifts from your loved one?

....

....

....

....

....

....

....

Special Places

The Lord had said to Abram, "Go from your country, your people and your father's household to the land I will show you."

GENESIS 12:1

Did you visit special places with your loved one? Perhaps you spent an afternoon in a nearby town or took a destination vacation thousands of miles away. Those experiences away from home together can have a precious space in our memories. I remember as a young woman, my mentor decided to take me out for high tea in the neighboring town. I had no idea what "high tea" meant and what a fancy occasion it would be, and I was not dressed up appropriately. I thought we were simply going out to lunch. I dressed in shorts and flip-flops for a California summer day. When we arrived, I found myself thankful for the long white linen tablecloth I could drape over my bare legs. I was quite embarrassed, but my mentor did not seem ashamed to be with me. The memory stands out to me about how she accepted me and gently taught me by example along the way.

What was a special visit or vacation that you took with your loved one? What were some highlights of this visit? Looking back, what did you learn about your loved one or your relationship in those times?

_____

_____

_____

_____

_____

_____

What are some of the places that you visited or traveled to with your loved one? Are there other places that you hoped to go? How will you honor the memory of your loved one regarding these unfulfilled goals or dreams?

_____

_____

_____

_____

_____

_____

Favorite Foods

Nehemiah said, "Go and enjoy choice food and sweet drinks, and send some to those who have nothing prepared. This day is holy to our Lord. Do not grieve, for the joy of the Lord is your strength."

NEHEMIAH 8:10

In this verse, the people were celebrating the reading of the Book of the Law of God. Delicious, rich food usually accompanies days of celebration and joy. Every family has its favorite food traditions for celebratory times. Sometimes the preparation of the food is as much to be celebrated as enjoying the feast.

Think about the food memories you have with your loved one. One of my stepmom's specialties was making carrot cake from scratch with cream cheese frosting. My mentor used to wait for her brother to send pecans from Texas so she could make pecan pie for Christmas. Whenever I grow eggplant in the garden, I think of my grandma who first introduced me to eggplant parmesan. A loved one gave me a cast iron Dutch oven with the spirit of good taste. No matter what I cook in that pot, it comes out delicious. Food brings back memories of special occasions and special people.

Take a moment to recall the foods and food rituals you associate with your loved one. What were some of their favorite foods? Did they prepare favorite dishes that you enjoyed? What did you prepare especially for them?

Have you enjoyed these foods since your loved one passed? How do you honor your loved one when you prepare or eat foods that remind you of them?

Observing Grief

Looking Back Exercise:

If your loved one lived with you, take a walk around your home. Perhaps there are places they claimed as a workspace, a closet full of their belongings, or their seat in the living room. Consider any changes in your home you have not previously been ready to make. Commit to an action this week to go through that closet, work area, or pile of paperwork. Spend 30 minutes a day on the task. Make some progress each day.

If your loved one did not live with you, where or when do you most feel their absence? Have you avoided places, conversations, or other experiences you associate with them and, as such, with the pain of losing them? Take a step this week to challenge your reluctance. Face and acknowledge the feelings that urge you toward avoidance.

Sometimes it feels better to ignore places or tasks that stir up too much pain. What specifically do you need help with? Is it help with moving things? A friend to provide emotional support? Maybe you need grace to be willing to do things you have avoided. Write down your prayer asking God for His help as you challenge yourself.

Looking Forward Exercise:

Are there any adjustments in your physical environment that you are ready to make? What challenge could you give yourself to reclaim places from your former life or complete tasks you have put off? If you are ready to move forward, invite a friend over to talk about the significance of the tasks or places you have avoided. Perhaps you know someone who is further along the road of grief who would understand what you are going through because they have had to face similar issues.

Father God, there are changes I need to make, but sometimes I don't know where to start. Please give me the courage and willingness to move in a positive direction for the healing of my life. Let my heart be renewed in hope and purpose. Help me make the needed changes so I can be prepared for the next steps You have for me.

Anniversaries, Birthdays, and Holidays

There is a time for everything, and a season for every activity under the heavens.

ECCLESIASTES 3:1

In relation to grief, special dates are hard. We miss the ones who witnessed our life's most important moments. One way to buffer the pain of significant dates is to prepare for them rather than just let them happen to you. You can ask for what you want and need. Some families create new traditions in honor of their loved ones. Others purposefully maintain the familiar traditions as a way to honor shared experiences with loved ones who have passed. For 15 years of holidays after my stepmom died, one of us daughters always made Mom's lemon-lime Jell-O with cream cheese salad in her Bundt cake mold. Sometimes the Jell-O didn't have time to fully set in the refrigerator, and it rarely flipped out of the pan properly, the way it did for Mom. Even if the Jell-O didn't always bond with the cream cheese, as we passed the jiggling dish around the table, the experience bonded us to Mom and to one another in our family traditions.

Creating your holiday plan can keep you from getting emotionally overwhelmed and may help avoid misunderstandings with family members. What significant dates are approaching? What ideas do you have for honoring your loved one on these dates? Who can help you?

....

....

....

....

....

....

Write down some of your favorite memories from anniversaries, birthdays, holidays, and other special occasions. What happened and how did you feel at the time? Who can you share these stories with?

....

....

....

....

....

....

....

Self-Care

. . . there by his head was some bread
baked over hot coals, and a jar of water.
He ate and drank and then lay down
again. The angel of the Lord came back
a second time and touched him and said,
"Get up and eat, for the journey is too
much for you." So he got up and ate and
drank. Strengthened by that food, he
traveled forty days and forty nights . . .

1 KINGS 19:5–8

Here we see Elijah exhausted, discouraged, and alone after
running from Jezebel, who threatened to kill him. Have you ever
been stuck in a place where all you could do was sleep? Grief
takes a toll on us, physically and mentally. Sometimes we need
to focus on the basics, like food and rest, just to keep going.
But self-care also means nurturing activities to relieve stress.
These may include exercising, taking a shower, getting a haircut
or a massage, going on a trip outdoors, talking with a friend or
counselor, or scheduling overdue doctor appointments. If you
identify with what the angel said to Elijah, "The journey is too
much for you," take some time to pray and ask God for help. If
you notice difficulty with self-care tasks for more than a few
days, please talk to a friend or counselor.

Do you prioritize self-care? How often do you set aside time to focus on your basic needs? What kinds of things do you do to nurture yourself?

Have you neglected any important care for yourself, such as doctor appointments, meal planning, or hygiene? If so, consider why certain tasks have been difficult for you. What steps could you take this week to improve your self-care?

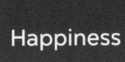

Happiness

When times are good, be happy;
but when times are bad, consider this:
God has made the one as well as the
other. Therefore, no one can
discover anything about their future.

ECCLESIASTES 7:14

The dictionary defines happiness as a state of well-being and contentment. The definition of grief includes "deep sadness." The two seem mutually exclusive, yet both are a part of our lives. When we are enjoying seasons of happiness, rarely do we contemplate that these seasons do not last forever. If we did, it would likely cloud over that pleasure. Sometimes, only in grief can we fully appreciate the blessings we had as we look back.

You didn't just lose your loved one. You lost who you were in that unique relationship that cannot be replaced. You laughed at their jokes, or they laughed at yours. There were mutual understandings that others didn't share. There were memories exclusive to your relationship. Your life included familiar patterns of connection that were precious to you. Take time to remember the experiences of happiness and contentment you shared with your loved one. Thank God for these memories.

Reread the scripture verse above. What does it mean to you that "no one can discover anything about their future"? Write down your reflections.

....

....

....

....

....

....

....

Reflect and write about three of your happiest memories with your loved one. What made these times special to you? To them?

....

....

....

....

....

....

....

An Appointed Time in History

*From one man he made all the
nations, that they should inhabit
the whole earth; and he marked out
their appointed times in history and
the boundaries of their lands.*

ACTS 17:26

Take a moment to meditate on this week's verse and how God
appoints every person for their time in history and where they
will live. That means that God knows who will live near you
and who you will know and what season in their appointed
time in history you will know them. When I returned from a
year of missions work in Mexico, I went to Nebraska to work
at a Gospel Rescue Mission. One of the first people I met was
assigned to train me. She has had a significant influence on my
life during our friendship of 30 years. I call her my adopted
mom. In the ups and downs of life she has been wonderful,
listening to me, encouraging me, and praying for me. She taught
me how to see things from God's perspective and to trust that
He is working out His plan.

Reflect on your relationship with your loved one in your *appointed time in history*. What is significant about the influence they had on your life? What did they teach you? How did they help you? How did you influence them?

_____

_____

_____

_____

_____

Consider other significant people in your life, who may be living or deceased, and what you imagine God's purposes to be in the *appointed time in history* you have shared together. Write about your reflections.

_____

_____

_____

_____

_____

_____

The Joy of Reunion

And I heard a loud voice from the throne
saying, "Look! God's dwelling place is
now among the people, and he will dwell
with them. They will be his people, and
God himself will be with them and be
their God. He will wipe every tear from
their eyes. There will be no more death
or mourning or crying or pain, for the
old order of things has passed away."
He who was seated on the throne said,
"I am making everything new!" Then
he said, "Write this down, for these
words are trustworthy and true."

REVELATION 21:3–5

God is moved by our pain and our tears. He is planning a day
when "there will be no more death or mourning or crying or
pain." All the things we suffer in this life, such as pain, illness,
rejection, difficult relationships, unmet needs, or abandonment,
prepare us to long for heaven more. We were not created to be
satisfied long-term by life on earth in what the Bible refers to as
"the old order of things" that will pass away. We were created
to crave fellowship with God for eternity. Your grief will not be
this intense forever. Consider using this season of grief to meditate on God's promises for your future with Him. Imagine the
pain resolved and the joy of your reunion with loved ones.

What do you imagine that day will be like for you when God makes everything new? Have a conversation with God about what you are looking forward to.

How can you let your pain turn you toward God more? What other reflections do you have on this scripture verse?

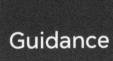

Guidance

Let the morning bring me word of
your unfailing love, for I have put my
trust in you. Show me the way I should
go, for to you I entrust my life.

PSALM 143:8

After a major loss, many of our plans get rearranged or
destroyed. If we planned life with a spouse who died, then
we—alone—may not want to or be able to do the things we
planned. Other losses could change our motivation to do things
we once looked forward to doing. The loss of a loved one can
make the thought of going on vacation feel distressing. If you
lost a pet, it may be difficult to go out for a walk without them.
It may be challenging to find motivation for going to work when
your purpose and plans feel thwarted. With life and emotions
thrown into chaos, we may not know what to do, or even what
we want to do tomorrow. The options can feel confusing or
unpleasant. Between considering what is best for us and what
we really want, we can become paralyzed with indecisiveness in
the process. When overwhelmed by grief, we may not even trust
our own thoughts. We can pray and ask the Lord to show us the
direction we should go.

As you read and reflect on this scripture verse, what are your thoughts? Are you able to turn toward God and trust in His unfailing love? If, right now, you are not able to do this, reflect on why.

_____

_____

_____

_____

_____

_____

What are some things you want to ask God's guidance for?

_____

_____

_____

_____

_____

_____

_____

_____

Where, O Death, Is Your Sting?

When the perishable has been clothed with the imperishable, and the mortal with immortality, then the saying that is written will come true: "Death has been swallowed up in victory." "Where, O death, is your victory? Where, O death, is your sting?" The sting of death is sin, and the power of sin is the law. But thanks be to God! He gives us the victory through our Lord Jesus Christ.

1 CORINTHIANS 15:54–57

A day is coming when the pain of death and grief will be erased. Right now, death still stings, but the pain won't last forever. On that coming day, "there will be no more death or mourning or crying or pain" (Revelation 21:4). God promises to take it all away. We who have been touched by this pain will be forever grateful that we never have to experience it again. In the meantime, we let this hope remind us that the pain is temporary. God has a plan to overcome everything that distresses us today.

What do you imagine it will be like to experience the victory described in these verses? By faith, will you make the Apostle Paul's words your declaration? "Thanks be to God! He gives us the victory through our Lord Jesus Christ."

_____

_____

_____

_____

_____

_____

_____

What other thoughts or reflections do you have on these scripture passages?

_____

_____

_____

_____

_____

_____

_____

Comforting Others

Praise be to the God and Father of our Lord Jesus Christ, the Father of compassion and the God of all comfort, who comforts us in all our troubles, so that we can comfort those in any trouble with the comfort we ourselves receive from God. For just as we share abundantly in the sufferings of Christ, so also our comfort abounds through Christ.

2 CORINTHIANS 1:3–5

By the time I was six years old my parents were separated, and when I was eight, we moved 2,500 miles from my mother. I didn't see her for several years. Today I look back and recognize that, by such a separation, I experienced grief as a child. As a young adult working in a Gospel Rescue Mission, I met a woman who told me about horrible abuse from family members in her childhood. Even though my suffering didn't come anywhere close to what she had experienced, I realized that day that my pain could help me empathize with what she had suffered. I began to understand God's plan for me to help others heal. Having a measure of healing for my pain, I could "comfort those in any trouble with the comfort [I received] from God."

What do you believe God wants you to understand from this week's reading? Write your reflections.

In what ways have you experienced God's comfort in your troubles? What have you learned that could be helpful to someone experiencing a similar loss?

Restoration

I will repay you for the years the locusts have eaten . . . You will have plenty to eat, until you are full, and you will praise the name of the Lord your God, who has worked wonders for you; never again will my people be shamed.

JOEL 2:25–26

God is in the business of restoring broken things; He heals the brokenhearted (Psalm 147:3); He removes our transgressions as far as the east is from the west (Psalm 103:12); He makes the barren woman the happy mother of children (Isaiah 49:21); He sets captives free (Isaiah 61:1); He turns mourning into dancing and sorrow into joy (Psalm 30:11); He blessed the latter part of Job's life more abundantly than the first part (Job 42:12); He heals the sick (Exodus 23:25); He raises the dead (2 Corinthians 4:14); He feeds the hungry (Matthew 6:33–34); He gives justice to the oppressed (Luke 18:7); He provides love to drive out fear (1 John 4:18); and much, much more.

Whatever need you have, He desires to provide the answer. It doesn't always look like what we expect, but He is faithful to His promises. We may not understand what He is doing for us in difficult circumstances, but He loves us and has good plans for us. He encourages us to ask and keep on asking for the restoration, healing, and wholeness we need (Matthew 7:7–8).

Can you recall other scriptures about God providing for various needs? Consider looking up and meditating on the verses noted above. Record your reflections.

What are some of the needs you have right now? Ask the Lord for the specific things or the work of His grace that would meet your needs.

Observing Grief

Looking Back Exercise:

Wherever you are in your experience of grief, you are not in the same place as where you started. Do you remember feeling overwhelmed, the questions about stages of grief, the tears, the fatigue, the mental fog? Write a letter to your younger self, the part of you who started this journey of grief. Write about wise advice for getting through the first few weeks and months after your loss. What do you wish you knew then? What encouragement and hope would have been helpful? What are some practical tips you would offer? These tips and encouragements may also be useful to someone you know now going through the disorienting experience of grief for the first time.

Thank God for the lessons learned on this journey. Ask Him to show you with whom you could share some encouragement and practical help. Make note of the spontaneous thoughts and impressions that come to mind.

Looking Forward Exercise:

Write another letter to your future self 12 months from now. Write about what you hope life will look like for you then. Where will you be living? Will you have learned a new skill? What will you have done or accomplished by then? What will you be looking forward to?

Date your letter and place it in an envelope along with the letter about practical tips and advice for dealing with grief. Tuck it away somewhere safe. Set a reminder on your smartphone, computer, or calendar for a date a year from today to remember where to find your letter so you can reread it then.

Lord, thank You for walking with me through the trials of grief. You are a friend that sticks closer than a brother (Proverbs 18:24). I pray that You will transform my sorrow into comfort for me and others. Let my loss result in bearing fruit for eternity as others are helped by what I've learned.

CLOSING PRAYER

Wow, you made it! Take some time to reflect on the moments you have shared with the Lord in this grief journal. You are not the same person today as when you started this journey. Congratulations for taking this path through the scriptures, hearing God's voice, and letting Him minister to your soul. This is not the end. The Lord wants to continue to nurture your soul as you adjust your life to all the changes that have occurred.

Lord Jesus, thank You for joining me on this journey. Thank You for Your peace and comfort. Thank You for drawing me close to You in my time of need. Please give me the opportunity to share with others the hope and healing You have shared with me. Continue to show me Your presence and grace as I walk on the path that You have for me, in Your name. Amen.

RESOURCES

BOOKS

A Grief Observed by C.S. Lewis

Healing Your Grieving Heart: 100 Practical Ideas by Alan D. Wolfelt

Healing Your Holiday Grief: 100 Practical Ideas for Blending Mourning and Celebration during the Holiday Season by Alan D. Wolfelt

My Dream of Heaven: A Nineteenth Century Spiritual Classic by Rebecca Ruter Springer

On Grief and Grieving: Finding the Meaning of Grief through the Five Stages of Loss by Elisabeth Kübler-Ross and David Kessler

Parts Work: An Illustrated Guide to Your Inner Life by Tom Holmes, Lauri Holmes, and Sharon Eckstein

The Grief Recovery Handbook by John W. James and Russell Friedman

The Grief Recovery Handbook for Pet Loss by Russell Friedman, Cole James, and John W. James

When Your Pet Dies: A Guide to Mourning, Remembering and Healing by Alan D. Wolfelt

WEBSITES AND ORGANIZATIONS FOR GRIEVERS

750words.com

Encourages participants to write daily in an encrypted, secure website.

CompassionateFriends.org

Support for bereaved families after the death of a child.

GriefRecoveryMethod.com

Group and one-on-one support programs offered in person and online.

GriefShare.org

Grief support groups offered by local churches.

Meetup.com

Find and join groups locally and online related to your personal interests.

RainbowsBridge.com

Support for pet loss.

Stages-of-Grief-Recovery.com

Free resources and tips for dealing with grief available at the author's website.

WingsForWidows.org

Connect with free services for widows and widowers from financial planners to help sort out financial matters after a spouse dies.